A Guide for Using

# *Miss Nelson Is Missing!*
# *and Other*
# *Miss Nelson Books*

in the Classroom

*Based on the books written*
*by Harry Allard and James Marshall*

*This guide written by **Mary Bolte***

**Teacher Created Materials, Inc.**
6421 Industry Way
Westminster, CA 92683
www.teachercreated.com
©2000 Teacher Created Materials
Made in U.S.A.
**ISBN 1-57690-641-8**

*Edited by*
*Lorin Klistoff, M.A.*

*Illustrated by*
*Wendy Chang*

*Cover Art by*
*Wendy Chang*

# Table of Contents

# Introduction

A good book can touch the lives of children like a good friend. The pictures, words, and characters can inspire young minds as they turn to literary treasures for companionship, recreation, comfort, and guidance. Great care has been taken in selecting the books and unit activities that comprise the primary series of Literature Units.

This unit is primarily concerned with the book *Miss Nelson Is Missing!* but activities are included for two other books, *Miss Nelson Is Back* and *Miss Nelson Has a Field Day*. These two books provide further amusing adventures at the Horace B. Smedley School.

Teachers who use this literature unit to supplement their own valuable ideas can plan the activities, using one of the following methods.

## Sample Lesson Plan

The Sample Lesson Plan on page 4 provides the teacher with a specific set of lesson plan suggestions. Each of the lessons can take from one to several days to complete and can include all or some of the suggested activities. Refer to the Suggestions for Using the Unit Activities on pages 8–10 for information relating to the unit activities.

## Unit Planner

For the teacher who wishes to tailor the suggestions on pages 8–10 in a format other than that prescribed in the Sample Lesson Plan, a blank unit planner is provided on page 5. On a specific day, you may choose the activities you wish to include by writing the activity number or a brief notation about the activity. Space has been provided for reminders, comments, and other pertinent information relating to each day's activities. Reproduce copies of the Unit Planner as needed.

# Sample Lesson Plan

## Lesson 1

- With your students, read Getting to Know the Author and Illustrator and Getting to Know the Books on pages 6 and 7.
- Do Before the Book activities on page 8.
- Read the story *Miss Nelson Is Missing*! for enjoyment.

## Lesson 2

- Introduce the vocabulary on page 8 and complete Into the Book, activity 1.
- Reread the story, listening for vocabulary words.
- Retell the story using Into the Book, activity 2, including questions on page 15.
- Complete Acting Like Antonyms! on page 19.
- Create paper airplanes by completing Kids and Planes on page 27.
- Discuss the importance of rules. Then have students complete Ruling the Room on page 23.
- Complete What Would You Do? on page 24.
- Discuss how math can be fun and complete It's in the Bag! on page 26.

## Lesson 3

- Discuss substitute teachers and complete The Substitute on page 20.
- Discuss the differences between Smedley School and the students' school. Complete Compare Schools on page 22.
- Review writing names in ABC order and complete Get It in Order! on page 21.
- Discuss the importance of seating charts. Complete Seating Chart for Room 207 on page 25.

- Complete Butterflies, Mars, or Sharks? on page 28.
- Begin writing the reader's theater script on page 46.
- Make masks to show characters' feelings using Masks! Masks! Masks! on page 39.

## Lesson 4

- Continue to write and finish the reader's theater script.
- Create book covers using The New Substitute on page 33. Then write a story about the new substitute.
- Discuss a detective's job and its requirements. Complete Get a Clue! on page 32.
- Complete and practice the song, "I'll Never Tell," on page 35. Write a sequel to this song as described on page 10, Into the Book, activity 10.

## Lesson 5

- Practice the reader's theater script.
- Work in groups to make the stick puppets and puppet theaters on pages 16–18.
- Locate the different states and capitals around Texas using the map on page 29. Then play the game, Name That State!, on pages 30 and 31.
- Complete Faces Show Feelings on page 34.

## Lesson 6

- Practice the song and reader's theater script using puppets, puppet theaters, or masks.

- Before an audience, perform the reader's theater presentation and song.

# Unit Planner

| Unit Activities | Unit Activities |
|---|---|
| Date: | Date: |
| Notes: | Notes: |
| Unit Activities | Unit Activities |
| Date: | Date: |
| Notes: | Notes: |
| Unit Activities | Unit Activities |
| Date: | Date: |
| Notes: | Notes: |

# Getting to Know the Author and Illustrator

## Harry Allard

Harry Allard was born in 1928 in Evanston, Illinois, and graduated from Northwestern University. He served in the Korean War and later went to live in Paris. He obtained a Ph.D. in French from Yale in 1973. While teaching French at Salem State College in Massachusetts, he met James Marshall. They worked together on many projects until James Marshall's death in 1992.

Writing came naturally for Harry Allard. He often collaborated with James Marshall, who illustrated many of his popular children's books, including the *Miss Nelson* series. Revision and refinement played an important role in the success of their books. Harry Allard believed in simplicity and rhythm when expressing words.

## James Marshall

James Marshall was born in 1942 in San Antonio, Texas. He attended various colleges and graduated from Connecticut State College. While teaching Spanish and French at a private school, he continued his hobby of drawing and then illustrated books for Houghton Mifflin. Marshall always believed that a book must "move" to motivate the reader to read on to the next page. James Marshall's expressive illustrations created numerous and humorous children's books enjoyed by all ages.

6

# Getting to Know the Books

### *Miss Nelson Is Missing!*

*(Available in U.S.A., Houghton Mifflin Company, 1977; Canada, Thomas Allen & Son; UK, Cassell; AUS, Jackaranda Wiley)*

Bedlam and turmoil occur in Room 207 every day as students take advantage of their kind-hearted and meek teacher. Miss Nelson tries to control the class. Subsequently, she disguises herself as a mean substitute, Miss Viola Swamp, who rules the class with an "iron fist." The distressed students report Miss Nelson's disappearance to Detective McSmogg, but Miss Nelson quickly returns to her class of "perfect" students. The students are thrilled that Miss Swamp is gone as they exhibit their appreciation for their favorite teacher, Miss Nelson.

### *Miss Nelson Is Back*

*(Available in U.S.A., Houghton Mifflin Company, 1982; Canada, Thomas Allen & Son; UK, Cassell; AUS, Jackaranda Wiley)*

Once again, Miss Nelson is absent from the classroom. She is having her tonsils taken out, and the students are fearful that Miss Viola Swamp will once again return. Principal Blandsworth takes charge of the class. The students quickly become bored with his teaching techniques. They create a secret plan to disguise three of their classmates as Miss Nelson. The plan succeeds at convincing Mr. Blandsworth that their favorite teacher has returned. The students are soon to be surprised by the appearance of Miss Viola Swamp at the door. This hilarious sequel to *Miss Nelson Is Missing!* will convince the reader that Miss Nelson is still number one in Room 207.

### *Miss Nelson Has a Field Day*

*(Available in U.S.A., Houghton Mifflin Company, 1985; Canada, Thomas Allen & Son; UK, Cassell; AUS, Jackaranda Wiley)*

Miss Viola Swamp appears once again as the mean, substitute football coach. Miss Swamp revamps a losing Smedley Tornadoes football team of lazy, unmotivated youngsters. Her strict discipline soon gets the team in shape. Readers will be puzzled as they see Miss Nelson in the classroom and Coach Swamp on the field simultaneously. A unique ending to this story adds, once again, to the fascination of Miss Nelson's adventures.

# Suggestions for Using the Unit Activities

Use some or all of the following suggestions to introduce your students to *Miss Nelson Is Missing!* and to expand their appreciation of the book through activities that cross the curriculum. The suggested activities have been divided into three sections to assist you in planning this literature unit.

Suggestions are arranged in the following sections:

- *Before the Book*: This section includes suggestions for preparing the classroom environment and the students for the literature to be read.
- *Into the Book*: This section has activities that focus on the book's content, characters, theme, etc.
- *After the Book*: This section extends the reader's enjoyment of the book.

## Before the Book

1. Before you begin the book, prepare the vocabulary cards, story questions, and sentence strips for the pocket chart activities. (See Into the Book section and the story questions on page 15.)

2. Read the information about the author Harry Allard and the illustrator James Marshall on page 6.

3. Set the stage for reading *Miss Nelson Is Missing!* by discussing the following questions:

   - What kinds of teachers do you respect?
   - What is a substitute teacher?
   - Have you ever been in a class with a substitute teacher? What was it like?

4. Display the cover of the book. Ask the following questions about the cover:

   - What do you see on the cover?
   - Why do you think most of the children are frowning?
   - What kind of class do you think this is?
   - Why do you think Miss Nelson is missing?
   - In what state is this school? How do you know that?

5. Introduce the other characters in the book—Miss Viola Swamp, the rowdy children, and Detective McSmogg.

6. Discuss the words *disciplined* and *undisciplined*.

## Into the Book

### 1. Pocket Chart Activity: Vocabulary Cards

After reading the book, discuss the meanings of the following words in context. Make copies of the pencil on page 14 and the sentence strips on page 13. Write the vocabulary words on the pencil and the definitions on the sentence strips. Display the words on the pencil in a pocket chart (page 11) and have students match the definitions with the words.

| Vocabulary Words | | | | | |
|---|---|---|---|---|---|
| misbehave | rude | refuse | ugly | witch | business |
| homework | detective | missing | secret | discouraged | change |

# Suggestions for Using the Unit Activities *(cont.)*

## Into the Book *(cont.)*

**2. Pocket Chart Activity:  Story Questions**

Develop critical thinking skills, using Story Questions on page 15.  The questions are based upon Bloom's Taxonomy and are provided for each level of Bloom's Levels of Learning.  Reproduce the notepad on page 14.  Write each question on a notepad and place it in the pocket chart.

**3. More Pocket Chart Activities**

- Brainstorm a list of sentences retelling the story.  Display them in order on the pocket chart.
- Put some quotations from the story on sentence strips.  Print the name of each speaker on a separate card.  Use them for a matching activity on the pocket chart.
- Write exclamations in the story on the sentence strips.  Cut them in half.  Then match the beginning of each exclamation with its appropriate ending.
- Discuss the italicized words.  Write the italicized words in the story on separate cards and their meanings on sentence strips.  Use them for a matching activity on the pocket chart.

**4. Stick Puppet Theaters**

Prepare the theaters following the directions and suggestions on page 16.  Allow students to construct the puppets on pages 17 and 18 by coloring, cutting, and gluing the puppets onto tongue depressors or craft sticks.

**5. Language Arts**

- **Acting Like Antonyms! (page 19)**

  Discuss the meaning of *antonym*.  Then have students review the directions and complete the activity.

- **The Substitute (page 20)**

  Students discuss feelings about substitute teachers.  Read and discuss the directions together. Have students complete the activity independently and then share their responses.

- **Get It in Order! (page 21)**

  Review writing names in ABC order by students' last names, using a class list.  Then describe the different features of each child's face.  Students complete the activity independently.

- **Compare Schools (page 22)**

  Study the illustrations in the book showing the Horace B. Smedley School.  Students write about the differences between their school and the Horace B. Smedley School.

- **Ruling the Room (page 23)**

  Students help Miss Nelson create some rules and consequences for the kids in Room 207.

- **What Would You Do? (page 24)**

  Read the three situations with the students and discuss possible solutions.  Children choose their own solutions and record them on their papers.

**6. Math**

- **Seating Chart for Room 207 (page 25)**

  Examine the seating chart for Room 207.  Then complete the activity together or individually. When finished, model the seating arrangements.

- **It's in the Bag! (page 26)**

  Read the scenario with the students.  Then have children play a bean game practicing odd and even numbers.

# Suggestions for Using the Unit Activities *(cont.)*

## Into the Book *(cont.)*

### 7. Science

- **Kids and Planes (page 27)**

  Discuss paper airplanes and practice folding paper to create different kinds of planes. Then read and follow the directions and compare this plane to the others. Practice flying the planes and share conclusions.

- **Butterflies, Mars, or Sharks? (page 28)**

  Discuss the difference between a fact and an opinion. Research facts about butterflies, Mars, and sharks. Have students share opinions about these three topics and complete the activity independently.

### 8. Social Studies

- **Name That State! (pages 29–31)**

  Study the map of Texas and its surrounding states on page 29. Students then use the blank map and cards on pages 30 and 31 to practice naming the states and their capitals.

- **Get a Clue! (page 32)**

  Discuss the career of a detective and compare it to other careers. Brainstorm ways a detective may solve a case using the "5 W" words. Then reread *Miss Nelson Is Missing*! and review the information needed to solve the case. Have students complete the bottom of the page independently. At the end, ask the students if they think Detective McSmogg solved the case.

### 9. Art

- **The New Substitute (page 33)**

  Talk about the characteristics of different real or imaginary substitute teachers and describe them using adjectives. Let the students pretend that they are to create a cover for a new book, *The New Substitute*. Students are to complete the activity and share with others.

- **Faces Show Feelings (page 34)**

  Students use their own faces to express feelings, such as happy, sad, excited, surprised, bored, etc. Study the faces of the kids in Room 207 and how they change when Miss Nelson leaves and Viola Swamp is in charge. Students will draw portraits of two boys and two girls from 207. Talk about how their expressions change.

### 10. Music

- **I'll Never Tell (page 35)**

  Sing "The Farmer in the Dell" to familiarize the students with the tune. Discuss Miss Nelson's comment "I'll never tell" at the end of the book and why she said it to herself with a smile. Then fill in the missing rhyming words to complete the song "I'll Never Tell." Sing it together. Students can collaborate and write a sequel song, "Miss Nelson, She Did Tell" to the same tune.

## After the Book

### 1. Culminating Activities

- **Reader's Theater Script (page 46)**

  Perform a play while minimizing the use of props, sets, costumes, or memorization. Students read the dialogue of the characters or narrate from the book or prepared script.

- **Alike and Different (page 47)**

  Compare the similarities and differences between two or three of the Miss Nelson stories.

# Pocket Chart Activities

## How to Make a Pocket Chart

If a commercial pocket chart is unavailable, you can make a pocket chart if you have access to a laminator. Begin by laminating a 24" x 36" (61 cm x 91 cm) piece of colored tagboard. Cut nine 2" x 20" (5 cm x 51 cm) or six 3" x 20" (8 cm x 51 cm) strips of clear plastic to use as pockets. Space the strips equally down the 36-inch (91-cm) length of the tagboard. Attach each strip with clear plastic tape along the sides and bottom. This will hold the sentence strips, word cards, etc., and can be displayed in a learning center or mounted on a chalk rail for use with a group. When your pocket chart is ready, use it to display sentence strips, vocabulary words, and question cards.

## How to Use the Pocket Chart

- On yellow or white paper, reproduce the pencil pattern on page 14. Make vocabulary cards as directed on page 8. Print the definitions on the sentence strips on page 13 for a matching activity. A sample chart is shown below.

- Print the names of the characters—Miss Nelson, Viola Swamp, the kids in Room 207, and Detective McSmogg—on the pencil pattern. Reproduce the notepad pattern on page 14. Write the quotations from the book on the notepad pattern. Match the quotations to the characters.

| definition or sentence | word |
|---|---|
| definition or sentence | word |
| definition or sentence | word |
| definition or sentence | word |
| definition or sentence | word |
| definition or sentence | word |

# Pocket Chart Activities *(cont.)*

## How To Use the Pocket Chart *(cont.)*

- Summarize the story in several sentences. The teacher can do this in advance or have the students help with this task. Write each sentence on a sentence strip. Students can then work alone or with a partner at a learning center to practice sequencing the sentence strips. As an extension, have students create their own mini-book by copying the sentences on sheets of paper stapled together. They can then illustrate each page.

- Reproduce several copies of the notepad pattern on page 14. Write the story questions on page 15 and the level of Bloom's Levels of Learning on each notepad pattern. The level of the question can be written at the top of the notepad. If desired, laminate each piece for durability.

### Examples

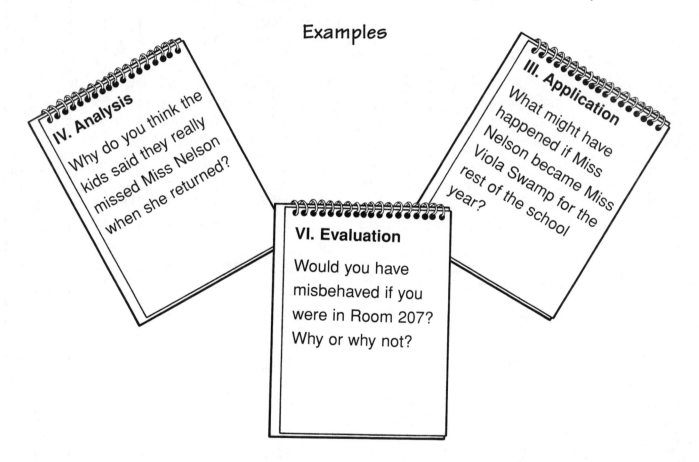

- After reading the story, use the story questions to provide opportunities for students to develop and practice higher-level, critical-thinking skills.

- Work together as a class or small group to write the answer to each question on a sentence strip. As an alternative, students can work on each question by themselves or with a partner.

- Divide the class into teams. Ask for a response to a question from one of the question cards. Teams score a point for each appropriate response. If you have also prepared question cards for the other Miss Nelson books, mix up the cards and ask team members to also name the story that relates to the question. Extra points can be awarded if a team member can correctly name the story, too.

# Sentence Strip Frames

# Pocket Chart Patterns

**Directions:** Duplicate these patterns, as needed, for use with the pocket chart activities on pages 11 and 12. Enlarge or reproduce the patterns to fit a particular activity.

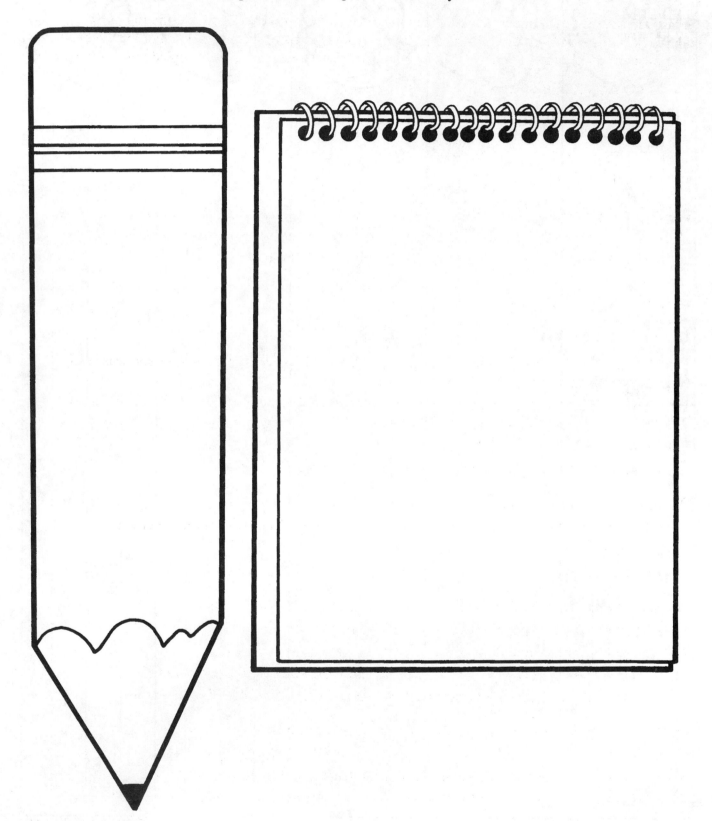

# Story Questions

Use the following questions for the suggested activities on pages 9 and 12. These questions are based on Bloom's Levels of Learning and help develop higher-level, critical-thinking skills. The questions promote discussion and provide excellent reasons for returning to the text to review the story.

Prepare the notepad pattern on page 14 and write a question on each notepad. At the top of the notepad, label the level. If desired, color-code the various levels of the questions. For example, all of the knowledge questions could be written on a notepad pattern which has been copied onto yellow paper.

### I. KNOWLEDGE *(ability to recall information)*
- Who is Miss Nelson?
- What does she do at her school?
- What kind of kids are in Room 207?
- Who is Miss Viola Swamp?

### II. COMPREHENSION *(ability to master basic understanding of information)*
- Why did the kids in Room 207 misbehave for Miss Nelson at the beginning of the book?
- Why did the kids in Room 207 behave for Miss Viola Swamp?
- What did the kids think happened to Miss Nelson?
- Why were the kids good when Miss Nelson returned?

### III. APPLICATION *(ability to do something new with information)*
- What do you think might have happened if the kids discovered that Miss Nelson was really Miss Viola Swamp?
- Why would you like or not like being one of the kids in Room 207?
- What might have happened if Miss Nelson became Miss Viola Swamp for the rest of the school year?
- How do you think Detective McSmogg got his name?

### IV. ANALYSIS *(ability to examine the parts of the whole)*
- Why do you think the kids said they really missed Miss Nelson when she returned?
- What were the two "secrets" in the story?
- At the end of the story, why do you think Miss Nelson said to herself, "I'll never tell"?

### V. SYNTHESIS *(ability to bring together information to make something new)*
- What might have happened if Detective McSmogg had found Miss Nelson?
- What would you have done if you were Miss Nelson?
- What might the kids have done if they had followed Miss Viola Swamp home?
- How would the kids have behaved if Miss Viola Swamp was Mr. Swamp instead?

### VI. EVALUATION *(ability to form and defend an opinion)*
- Would you have misbehaved if you were in Room 207? Why or why not?
- Do you think Miss Viola Swamp was a mean teacher? Why or why not?
- Would you always behave for Miss Nelson after she came back? Why or why not?

# Stick Puppet Theaters

Make a class set of puppet theaters (one for each student) or make one theater for every two to four students. The patterns and directions for making the stick puppets are on pages 17 and 18.

## Materials

- 24" x 36" (61 cm x 91 cm) pieces of colored poster board (enough for each student or group of students)

- markers, crayons, or paints

- scissors or a craft knife (knife for adult use only)

## Directions

1. Fold the poster board 8" (20 cm) in from each of the shorter sides. (See picture below.)

2. Cut a window in the front panel, large enough to accommodate three or four stick puppets.

3. Let the children personalize their own theaters.

4. Laminate the stick puppet theaters to make them more durable. You may wish to send the theaters home at the end of the year or save them to use year after year.

**Suggestions for Using the Puppets and the Puppet Theaters**

- Prepare the stick puppets. Use the puppets and the puppet theater with the reader's theater script developed from the story. See page 46 for how to develop you own reader's theater script. Students can create their own "children" stick puppets.

- Students can practice retelling the story using their own words or by reading the book.

- Students can make their own stick puppets to correspond with *Miss Nelson Is Back* or *Miss Nelson Has a Field Day*. Let them retell the stories using their own words or reading the books.

- Use the stick puppets when asking the questions on page 15. Students can hold up the stick puppets to answer the questions.

# Stick Puppet Patterns

**Directions:** Reproduce the patterns on tagboard or construction paper. Have students color the patterns. Cut them out along the dashed lines. Laminate them, if desired. To complete the stick puppets, glue each pattern to a tongue depressor or craft stick. Use the stick puppets with the puppet theaters or the reader's theater script.

**Miss Nelson**

**Detective McSmogg**

**Miss Viola Swamp**

# Stick Puppet Patterns *(cont.)*

See page 17 for directions.

**Kids in Room 207**

# Acting Like Antonyms!

When Miss Nelson taught the class, the children were terrible!  When Miss Viola Swamp taught the class, the children were wonderful!  *Terrible* and *wonderful* are antonyms.  *Antonyms* are words that are opposite in meaning.

**Directions:** Write the antonyms for each of the words below.  Use the word list to help you.

| Word List | | | | | |
|---|---|---|---|---|---|
| awful | sour | agree | wonderful | misbehave | polite |
| part | play | unload | shout | encourage | open |

1. behave    _____
2. load    _____
3. nice    _____
4. rude    _____
5. terrible    _____
6. whole    _____
7. shut    _____
8. refuse    _____
9. discourage    _____
10. whisper    _____
11. work    _____
12. sweet    _____

**Directions:** Use some of the words above to write a few sentences about Miss Nelson's or Miss Swamp's class.

_____

_____

_____

_____

# The Substitute

Miss Viola Swamp was an unpopular substitute teacher. What are some traits of a well-liked substitute? Think of a substitute teacher whom you really liked. Then write a story about your experience.

Title: _____

By: _____

_____

_____

_____

_____

_____

_____

_____

_____

_____

_____

_____

_____

_____

# Get It in Order!

When Miss Viola Swamp substituted for Miss Nelson, she never called students by their names. Maybe she needed a class list.

**Directions:** On the class list below, write the names in ABC order by their last names. Next to each name, draw a portrait of that child's face.

| Class List | | |
| --- | --- | --- |
| Stephen Sanford | Anthony Morales | Daniel DeLeon |
| Sara Sutton | Haley Mekus | Kelly Tikado |
| Demarco Hill | Marina Beech | Tim Chang |

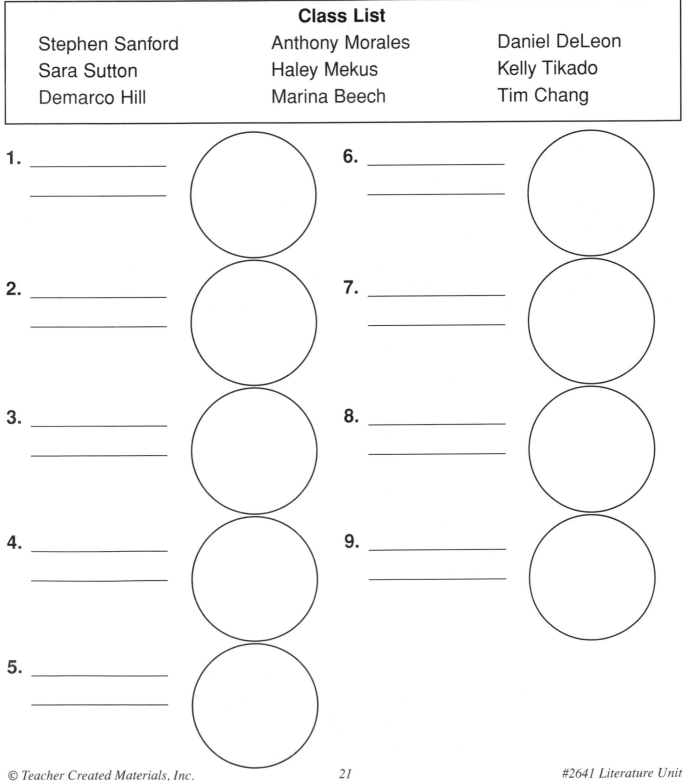

1. _____  _____

2. _____  _____

3. _____  _____

4. _____  _____

5. _____  _____

6. _____  _____

7. _____  _____

8. _____  _____

9. _____  _____

# Compare Schools

**Directions:** How is Horace B. Smedley School different from where you go to school? Look at the illustrations in the book showing the school and Room 207. Write how your school is different from the Horace B. Smedley School.

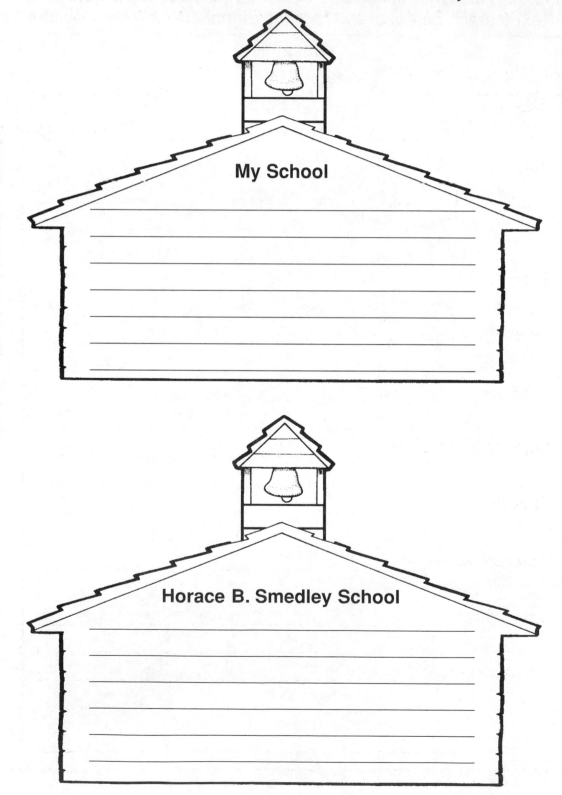

**My School**

**Horace B. Smedley School**

# Ruling the Room

The children in Room 207 misbehaved with Miss Nelson. They threw spitballs, flew paper airplanes, made faces, and did not listen to the teacher. Maybe Miss Nelson needed to make stricter rules.

**Directions:** Help Miss Nelson make five rules that you think are fair and would help bring the classroom back to order. Also, make a fair consequence (punishment) for each rule that is disobeyed.

**Rule 1:** _____
_____

*Consequence:* _____
_____

**Rule 2:** _____
_____

*Consequence:* _____
_____

**Rule 3:** _____
_____

*Consequence:* _____
_____

**Rule 4:** _____
_____

*Consequence:* _____
_____

**Rule 5:** _____
_____

*Consequence:* _____
_____

# What Would You Do?

Think about all the things that happen in the story. Miss Nelson disappears. A substitute teacher takes charge of the class. The students and a detective try to find Miss Nelson. Now consider what you might have done if you were one of the children in the class.

**Directions:** Write what you would do in each of the following situations. When you have finished writing your ideas, share some of them with your classmates.

---

**Situation 1**

Miss Nelson is reading a really good book, but some of the children are too noisy, and you cannot hear the story.

_____

_____

_____

---

**Situation 2**

Miss Viola Swamp assigns you so much work that you have no idea how you will ever finish it. In addition, she tells the class that anyone who does not finish his or her work will have to complete it during lunch, recess, or after school.

_____

_____

_____

---

**Situation 3**

You think about how awful the class has been to Miss Nelson. You know that if she ever returns, things should be different. What would you (and your classmates) do to make things better?

_____

_____

_____

# Seating Chart for Room 207

Miss Nelson had a seating chart for all the kids in her class. Her students tried to fool different substitutes by changing seats, but Miss Viola Swamp knew where they all sat.

**Directions:** Read the instructions and complete the seating chart. Write the children's names on their desks.

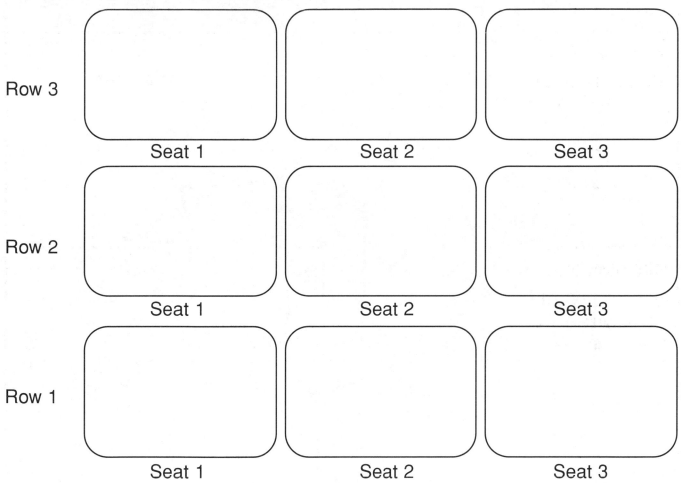

Row 3 — Seat 1 — Seat 2 — Seat 3

Row 2 — Seat 1 — Seat 2 — Seat 3

Row 1 — Seat 1 — Seat 2 — Seat 3

## Instructions

- Stephen Sanford sits in Row 3, Seat 1.
- Tim Chang sits in Row 1, Seat 2.
- Kelly Tikado sits in front of Stephen.
- Anthony Morales sits in Row 2, Seat 3.
- Haley Mekus sits between Kelly and Anthony.
- Marina Beech sits behind Anthony Morales.
- Sara Sutton sits in front of Kelly Tikado and next to Tim Chang.
- Demarco Hill sits behind Haley Mekus.
- Daniel DeLeon sits next to Tim Chang.

# It's in the Bag!

**Teacher Directions:** Set the stage for this activity by providing students with the following scenario. Then, introduce the bean math activity.

---

### Scenario

Miss Viola Swamp gave the children lots of classwork and homework. They probably had to write page after page of math problems. The kinds of problems Miss Viola Swamp assigned were not much fun. But math can be fun! Here is a math game to help you practice odd and even numbers. Can you think of other games that help you learn math and are fun at the same time? Share your ideas with your classmates.

---

## Materials

- 12 dried beans for each player
- small bags to hold the beans

## Objective

- practice odd and even numbers

## Where to Play

- at a table or the floor

## Number of Players

- two or more

## Directions

1. Give each player a bag containing 12 beans.

2. A player hides some beans in his or her fist and asks the next player, "Odd or even?"

3. If that next player guesses correctly, he or she wins the beans. If that player guesses incorrectly, he or she must give the same number of beans to the player who is holding the beans.

4. The second player then holds a certain number of beans in his or her hand and asks the third player the same question.

5. When a player loses all of his or her beans, he or she must drop out of the game.

(**Note:** You may wish to set a time limit. The person with the most beans at the end of this time period is declared the winner.)

# Kids and Planes

The kids in Miss Nelson's class like to make paper airplanes and fly them across the room, but where did this kind of plane originate?

Thousands of years ago, paper was invented in China, and later the first paper airplane was flown. Its wings give it lift so it can stay up in the air. The front of the wing is heavier and thicker than the back of the wing.

**Directions:** Read the directions below to make a paper airplane. Then fly the airplane outside.

**Materials:** a sheet of 8 ½" x 11" (22 cm x 28 cm) paper, paper clips, and tape

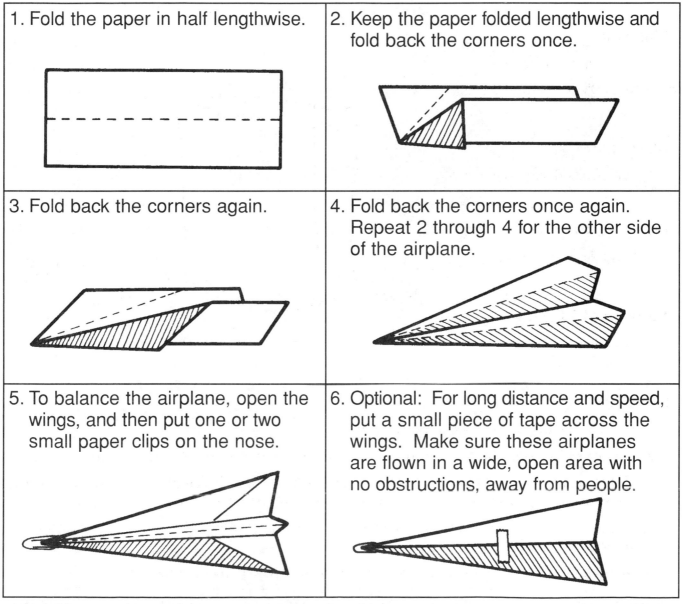

1. Fold the paper in half lengthwise.

2. Keep the paper folded lengthwise and fold back the corners once.

3. Fold back the corners again.

4. Fold back the corners once again. Repeat 2 through 4 for the other side of the airplane.

5. To balance the airplane, open the wings, and then put one or two small paper clips on the nose.

6. Optional: For long distance and speed, put a small piece of tape across the wings. Make sure these airplanes are flown in a wide, open area with no obstructions, away from people.

(**Variations:** Use colored paper for the airplane and decorate it. Try measuring the distances of each airplane flown.)

# Butterflies, Mars, or Sharks?

Was Miss Nelson's car lifted away by a swarm of mad butterflies?  Did Miss Nelson go to Mars?  Did a shark swallow Miss Nelson?  These are opinions.  An *opinion* is how or what you believe about something.

A butterfly is an insect with big, colorful wings.  Mars is the fourth planet in the solar system.  A shark is a large fish that can attack humans.  These are facts. A *fact* is true information about something.

**Directions:**  Write two facts and two opinions about each of the following subject areas:  butterflies, Mars, and sharks.

| | **Facts** | **Opinions** |
|---|---|---|
| 1. butterflies | | |
| 2. Mars | | |
| 3. sharks | | |

# Name That State!

Miss Viola Swamp loaded the children with homework. One assignment was to write the capitals of the states that are near Texas. Can you name the states and their capitals? How many of the states can you identify?

**Directions:** Study the labeled map below. Then use the blank map on page 30 and the cards on page 31 to practice locating the states around Texas and their capitals. (Once you have learned these states and their capitals, you can make up a game to learn the rest of the states.)

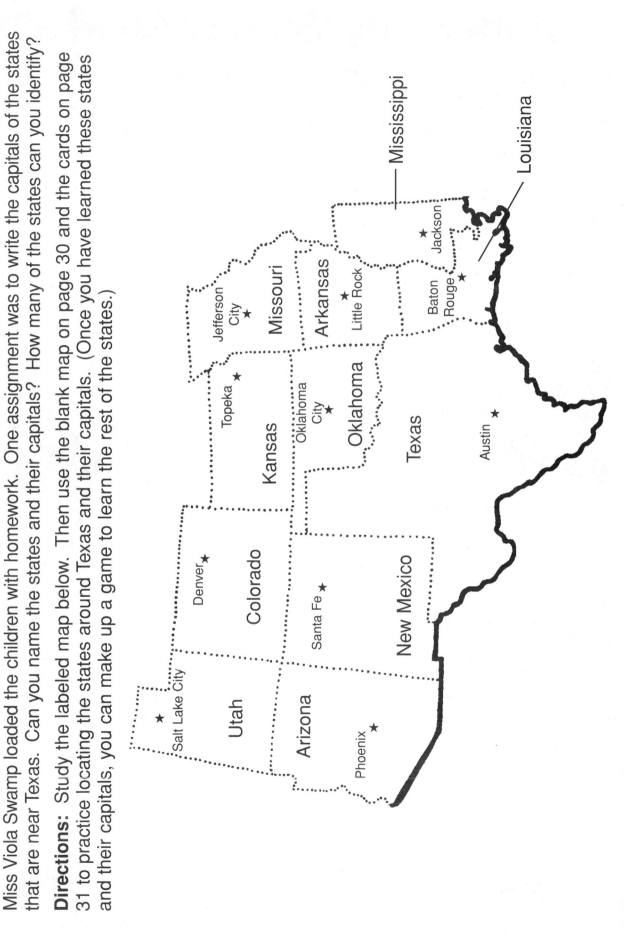

# Name That State! *(cont.)*

See page 29 for directions.

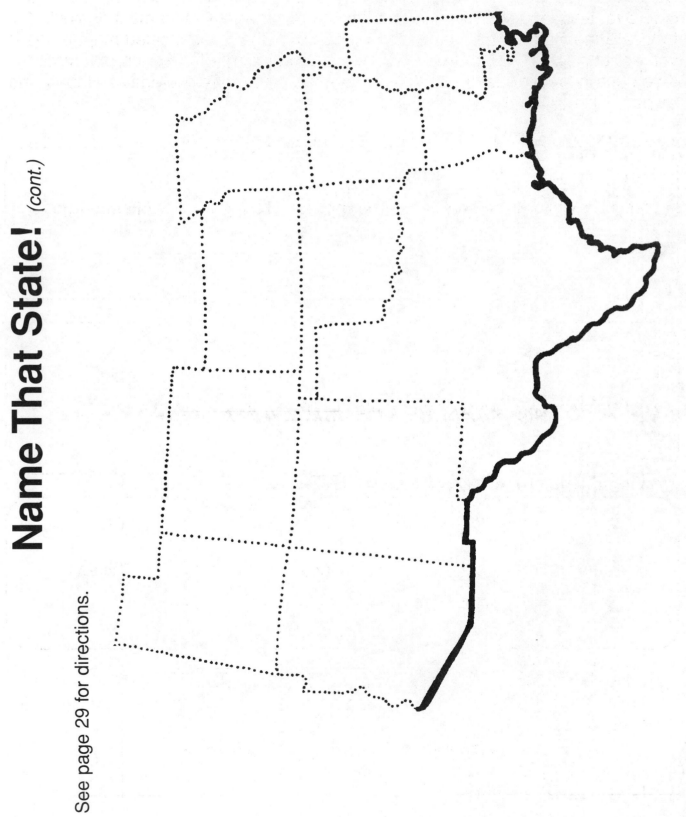

# Name That State! *(cont.)*

**Directions:** Cut out the cards and place them face down on a desk or table. Cover the labeled map (page 29) with a piece of construction paper. Turn one card over and read the state name. If you know the capital, name it as well. Try to locate the state on the blank map (page 30). Check the labeled map to see if you are correct. If you choose the correct state, place a marker on that state. If you are incorrect, place the state card in the face down pile again. Repeat the steps until you are able to identify each state.

| | | |
|---|---|---|
| New Mexico | Oklahoma | Mississippi |
| Arizona | Arkansas | Utah |
| Colorado | Louisiana | Texas |
| Kansas | Missouri | |

# Get a Clue!

A detective's job is to solve a case. Many times they ask themselves the "5 W" words (Who? What? Why? Where? When?).

**Directions:** Help Detective McSmogg solve his case of trying to find Miss Nelson. Answer the five questions, using complete sentences.

1. **WHO** reported the case? _____

   _____

2. **WHAT** was the problem? _____

   _____

3. **WHY** was it a problem? _____

   _____

4. **WHERE** did the problem occur? _____

   _____

5. **WHEN** did the problem occur? _____

   _____

**Directions**: Pretend you are Detective McSmogg and write about what you would do to solve this case. Use the back of this paper if you need more writing space.

_____

_____

_____

_____

_____

# The New Substitute

Miss Viola Swamp looked like a witch, and the kids thought she acted like one, too. Draw a picture of a "new" substitute on the book cover below. Then write some adjectives (words that describe nouns) that tell about the new substitute.

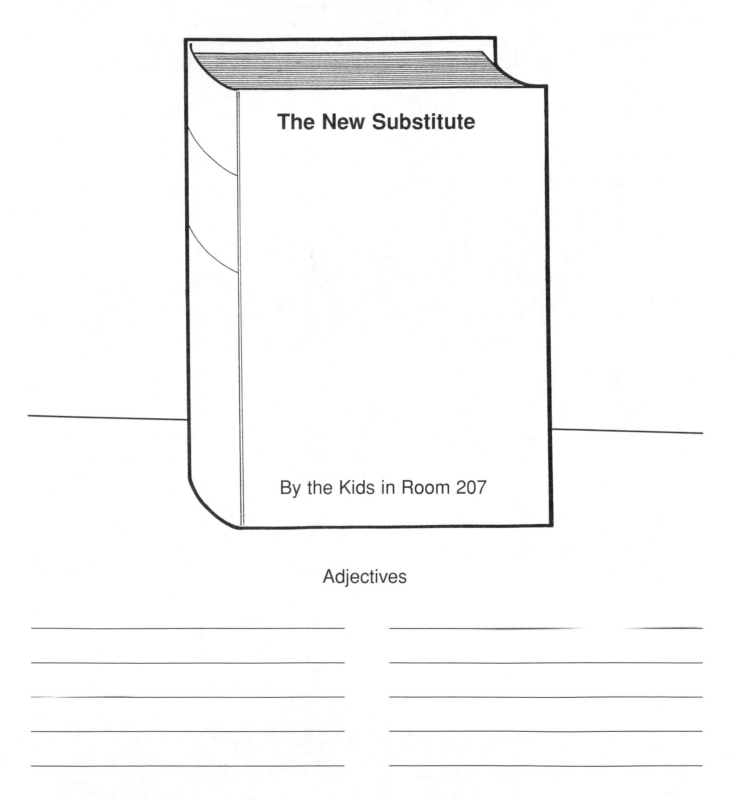

**The New Substitute**

By the Kids in Room 207

Adjectives

_____        _____

_____        _____

_____        _____

_____        _____

# Faces Show Feelings

A *portrait* can be a drawing, painting, or photograph of a person and usually shows just the face. Study the faces of all the children throughout the book, *Miss Nelson Is Missing!* The faces of some of the students in Miss Nelson's class changed when Miss Viola Swamp showed up.

**Directions:** In the picture frames below, draw some of the students' faces that showed their different feelings. Draw the children's faces when Miss Nelson was in the classroom and then when Miss Swamp was in the classroom.

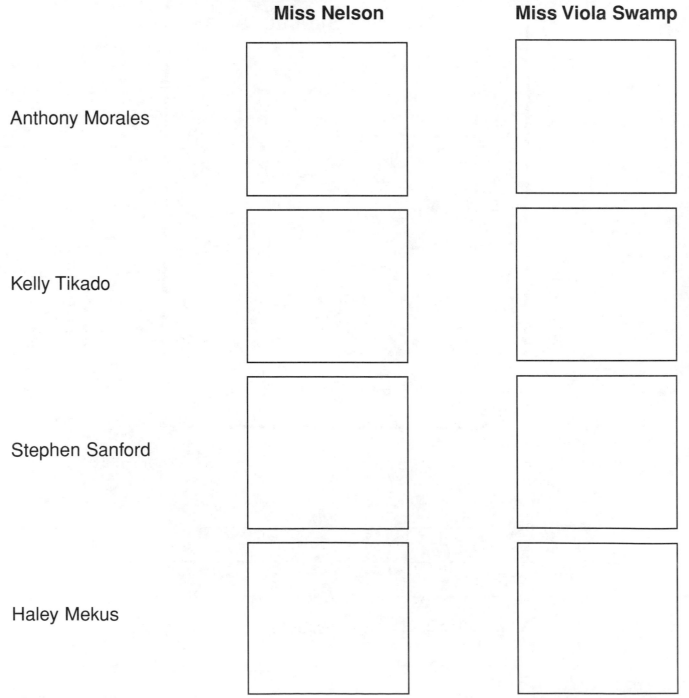

# I'll Never Tell

"I'll never tell," said Miss Nelson at the end of the book, as she sang a little song.

**Directions:** Using the word list below, add the correct rhyming words to the song, "I'll Never Tell." Then sing the song to the tune "The Farmer in the Dell."

| Word List | | | | | |
|---|---|---|---|---|---|
| shock wave | berserk | drill | rut | turn | tell |

**Verse 1**

Miss Nelson will never tell.

Miss Nelson will never _____.

That I am Miss Viola Swamp.

Miss Nelson will never tell.

**Verse 2**

I'll make those kids behave.

I'll make those kids behave.

I'll send them through a big _____.

I'll make those kids behave.

**Verse 3**

I'll give them lots of work.

I'll give them lots of work.

And enjoy watching them go _____.

I'll give them lots of work.

**Verse 4**

I'll tell them to sit still.

I'll tell them to sit still.

And then they'll have a spelling _____.

I'll tell them to sit still.

**Verse 5**

Their mouths will all be shut.

Their mouths will all be shut.

They'll feel like they are in a _____.

Their mouths will all be shut.

**Verse 6**

And when I do return.

Those kids will want to learn.

And they will be kind and take their

_____.

When Miss Nelson does return.

**Verse 7**

Miss Nelson will never tell.

Miss Nelson will never tell.

That I was Miss Viola Swamp.

Miss Nelson will never tell.

# Activities for Other Miss Nelson Books

## *Miss Nelson Is Back*

1. **Language Arts**
   - **A Diary for a Week (page 37)**
   Discuss a diary and its purpose. Students then each develop their own weekly diary.
2. **Math**
   - **Lunch at Lulu's (page 38)**
   The kids in Room 207 liked to go to Lulu's to "chow down" on their favorite foods. Students complete the activity independently.
3. **Art**
   - **Masks! Masks! Masks! (page 39)**
   Three kids in Room 207 disguised themselves as Miss Nelson with the help of a mask. Students learn more about masks as they complete this activity.
4. **Health**
   - **Add Some *Itis*! (page 40)**
   Read and discuss the information about suffixes, tonsils, and tonsillitis. Research other "itis" diseases and their causes. Complete the activity.

## *Miss Nelson Has a Field Day*

1. **Language Arts**
   - **Before and After (page 41)**
   Brainstorm adjectives that describe the Smedley Tornadoes team before and after Miss Viola Swamp came to the rescue. Then have students use the adjectives to write a newspaper article describing the amazing changes that took place with the team.
2. **Math**
   - **Jerseys for the Tornadoes (page 42)**
   The jerseys for the Tornadoes all look alike. So, each player has to have a number on his jersey to identify himself. Clues are given to find the correct numbers for each student.
   - **The Texas Ten (page 43)**
   Display win/loss records of different teams in the Texas Ten conference and discuss the sequencing. Then have students complete the activity independently.
   - **Football Points (page 44)**
   The Tornadoes scored zero points in the season until they played the Werewolves. Discuss football and how points are scored. Then complete the activity.
3. **Health**
   - **Get Immunized! (page 45)**
   Discuss the immunized diseases in the word search. Then students complete the word search.

## Culminating Activities

1. **Reader's Theater Script (page 46)**
   Perform a play while minimizing the use of props, sets, costumes, or memorization. Have students read the dialogue of the characters or narrate from the book or prepared script.
2. **Alike and Different (page 47)**
   Compare the similarities and differences between two or three of the Miss Nelson stories.

# A Diary for a Week

Miss Nelson told her students she would be gone from class for a week because she was having her tonsils out. Can you remember what you do in one week? A diary can help you remember what has happened each day.

**Directions:** Use seven copies of the "Daily Diary" to form a book. On each page, write about what you do each day of the week. (**Note:** Use one page for each day of the week.) At the end of the week, share your diary with a friend.

## Daily Diary

Name _____

Date _____

### This Is What Happened Today!

_____

_____

_____

_____

_____

_____

_____

_____

_____

_____

_____

_____

_____

# Lunch at Lulu's

The kids were all hungry after watching *The Monster That Ate Chicago* so they headed to Lulu's for some lunch. They quickly read the menu and ordered their lunches.

**Directions:** Read the menu and then solve the word problems.

### Lulu's Menu

| Sandwiches | | Snacks | | Drinks | |
|---|---|---|---|---|---|
| Texan Hamburger | $1.35 | Cowgirl Fries | $0.75 | Cowpoke Pop | $0.65 |
| Cowboy Chicken | $1.50 | Cowpoke Chips | $0.50 | Mustang Milk | $0.55 |
| Bronco Hotdog | $1.25 | Stetson Apple | $0.35 | Coyote Juice | $0.60 |
| | | Ranger Pretzel | $0.30 | | |

Lulu's Special Ice Cream Cones $0.25 a dip

1. Demarco Hill ordered 1 Texan Hamburger, 1 bag of Ranger Pretzels, and a Coyote Juice. How much did he spend?_____

2. Sara Sutton had a Bronco Hotdog, 4 dips of ice cream in a cone, and 1 Mustang Milk. What was the total cost of her lunch?_____

3. Tim Chang ordered 1 Cowboy Chicken, 2 Cowpoke Chips, and 1 Mustang Milk. How much did he have to pay?_____

4. Marina Beech had 1 Texan Hamburger, 1 Stetson Apple, 2 dips of ice cream in a cone, and 1 Cowpoke Pop. How much did Marina spend in all? _____

# Masks! Masks! Masks!

The kids in Room 207 grew tired of having Mr. Blandsworth as their substitute, so they created a new Miss Nelson "substitute." Three of the students disguised themselves in some big, old clothes, a wig, and a Miss Nelson mask. The mask helped convince their principal that Miss Nelson had returned.

Masks have been worn by people for thousands of years for different reasons. A mask is a cover worn over part or all of the face, as a disguise. There are many different ways to make masks. A simple way is to use a paper plate. Read and follow the directions and make masks for Miss Nelson, Miss Viola Swamp, and the kids in Room 207.

## Materials

- paper plates
- construction paper
- stapler
- scissors
- elastic
- tape
- markers or paints
- different-colored yarn
- glue

## Directions

1. On the paper plate, draw the face of Miss Nelson, Miss Viola Swamp, or one of the kids in Room 207.

2. Draw the eyes to match the eyes on your face, so you can see through the mask.

3. Cut out the eyes. Then draw and color the rest of the face.

4. Cut and glue colored construction paper or yarn onto your mask for hair.

5. Cut a strip of elastic and staple it to both sides of the mask.

6. Put on your mask and disguise yourself!

7. Use the masks to retell the story.

**Miss Nelson**

**Miss Viola Swamp**

# Add Some *Itis*!

Miss Nelson had to have her tonsils taken out. Tonsils are masses of soft tissue that are on each side of the throat. Sometimes they become infected and get larger in size. Then they are painful, and it is difficult to swallow. *Tonsillitis* is a word given to this disease, and often the tonsils are removed.

*Itis* is a suffix. A suffix can be one or more syllables that are added at the end of a word to form a new word and meaning. *Itis* means "inflammation of a body part." *Inflammation* means "heat, pain, redness, and swelling."

**Directions:** Read the description of the body parts. Then write their *itis* words from the word list.

---

**Word List**

appendicitis          bronchitis          gastritis          laryngitis

---

1. bronchial tubes—These are tiny tubes in the lungs through which air passes.

   _____

2. gastric—This term is anything that has something to do with the stomach.

   _____

3. larynx—This is known as the "voice box" and is located in the top part of the throat or windpipe that links the lungs with the mouth.

   _____

4. appendix—This is a small tube on the right side of the stomach and is attached to the beginning of the large intestine.

   _____

**Directions:** Choose one of the *itis* diseases and find out more about it. Write how you would feel if you had this disease. Use the back of this paper if you need more writing space.

_____

_____

_____

_____

# Before and After

Everyone at the Horace B. Smedley School was gloomy and depressed. Nobody smiled or laughed. Their school's football team, the Smedley Tornadoes, had not won a game all year. They were the worst team until Miss Viola Swamp came to their rescue.

**Directions:** Brainstorm adjectives to describe the Smedley Tornadoes before Miss Viola Swamp came to be the coach. Then describe the team after Miss Viola Swamp worked with them. Use the adjectives to help you write a newspaper article that tells of the amazing changes that took place with the Smedley Tornadoes.

**Before Miss Viola Swamp**                   **After Miss Viola Swamp**

_____       _____

_____       _____

_____       _____

_____       _____

### Extra! Extra!
### Smedley Tornadoes Take the Town!

_____

_____

_____

_____

_____

_____

_____

_____

_____

_____

_____

_____

# Jerseys for the Tornadoes

The jerseys (shirts) for the Tornadoes are green and yellow, and they all look alike. So, each player has to have a number on his jersey to identify him.

**Directions:** Read the clues below and write the correct numbers from the number list on each player's jersey.

## Clues

- The number on Stephen Sanford's jersey is less than 74 but 9 more than 54.
- Anthony Morales' number is more than 74 but 8 less than 89.
- Daniel DeLeon's jersey is an even number. It is the sum of 6 + 6 + 6 + 6 + 6.
- The number on Tim Chang's jersey is seven more than the letters in his name.
- Demarco Hill's number is a double digit and an even number.
- Miguel Peterson's jersey has a number that is one half of 100.
- The number on Mike Ling's jersey has a 7 in the ones' place and is 7 less than 14.
- Jason Greene's jersey has the number that is 22 more than the number on Miguel Peterson's jersey.

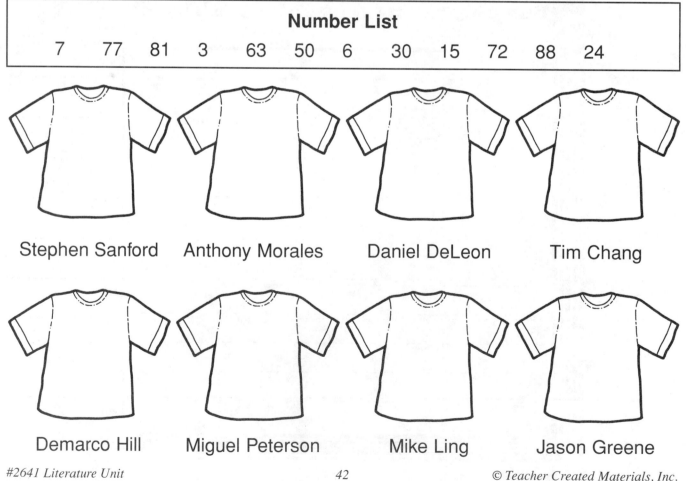

**Number List**

| 7 | 77 | 81 | 3 | 63 | 50 | 6 | 30 | 15 | 72 | 88 | 24 |

Stephen Sanford    Anthony Morales    Daniel DeLeon    Tim Chang

Demarco Hill    Miguel Peterson    Mike Ling    Jason Greene

# The Texas Ten

The Smedley Tornadoes were a very miserable football team. They had not scored a point or won a game all year. They had to play the Central Werewolves on Thanksgiving Day. They played in the Texas Ten Conference that included nine other teams.

**Directions:** Study the record of wins and losses for the ten teams. Then write the teams in order from the greatest number of wins to the least.

| Team | Wins | Losses | Team | Wins | Losses |
|------|------|--------|------|------|--------|
| Lasco Longhorns | 6 | 6 | Halliday Cowboys | 3 | 9 |
| Smedley Tornadoes | 0 | 12 | Central Werewolves | 12 | 0 |
| Terrell Wranglers | 8 | 4 | Spindletop Oilers | 9 | 3 |
| Estrada Broncos | 5 | 7 | Diablo Rangers | 7 | 5 |
| Anderson Mustangs | 11 | 1 | Woodland Bulldogs | 10 | 2 |

## THE TEXAS TEN

| | Team | Wins | Losses |
|---|------|------|--------|
| 1. | _____ | _____ | _____ |
| 2. | _____ | _____ | _____ |
| 3. | _____ | _____ | _____ |
| 4. | _____ | _____ | _____ |
| 5. | _____ | _____ | _____ |
| 6. | _____ | _____ | _____ |
| 7. | _____ | _____ | _____ |
| 8. | _____ | _____ | _____ |
| 9. | _____ | _____ | _____ |
| 10. | _____ | _____ | _____ |

# Football Points

The Smedley Tornadoes always tried to score points in their football games but had no luck.  In their Texas Ten games, points were scored in the following four ways:

| | |
|---|---|
| 6 points (touchdown) | The player carries the ball into the opposing team's end zone. |
| 1 point (one pointer) | A player kicks the ball through the goal posts after a touchdown. |
| 2 points (two pointer) | A pass or run over the goal is completed after a touchdown. |
| 3 points (field goal) | A player kicks the ball between the goal posts from the field.  This does not happen after a touchdown. |

**Directions:**  Read and solve the word problems about the points scored in some of the Texas Ten games.

1. The Tornadoes played the Anderson Mustangs, and the score was 14 to 0. How many touchdowns and one pointers did the Mustangs score?

   _____ touchdowns                    _____ one pointers

2. The Oilers beat the Tornadoes 16 to 0.  How many touchdowns and two pointers did the Oilers score?

   _____ touchdowns                    _____ two pointers

3. Once again, the Tornadoes lost a game.  This time they were defeated by the Halliday Cowboys, 24 to 0, by scoring only touchdowns.  How many touchdowns did the Cowboys score?

   _____ touchdowns

4. The Estrada Broncos beat the Tornadoes 15 to 0 by kicking only field goals. How many field goals did they kick?

   _____ field goals

5. The Tornadoes did great in their last game against the Central Werewolves. They won 77 to 3.  How many touchdowns and one pointers did the Tornadoes score?

   _____ touchdowns                    _____ one pointers

# Get Immunized!

Coach Armstrong was the coach of the Smedley Tornadoes, the worst football team in the state of Texas.  Luckily for the team, he got the measles.  Coach Armstrong must not have been immunized.  *Immunized* means to be protected from a disease through pills, shots, or serums (liquid medicine).

**Directions:**  Listed below are different diseases for which children who are six years old have been immunized.  Find the words in the word search.

| Word Search List | | | | |
|---|---|---|---|---|
| chicken pox | diptheria | hepatitis | measles | meningitis |
| mumps | polio | rubella | tetanus | whooping cough |

| | | | | | | | | | | | |
|---|---|---|---|---|---|---|---|---|---|---|---|
| m | u | m | p | s | d | m | u | n | s | z | t | h |
| e | a | p | o | l | i | o | p | w | p | r | g | e |
| n | c | w | k | o | p | o | o | h | x | u | z | p |
| i | r | t | b | r | t | q | n | o | o | b | f | a |
| n | u | e | j | d | h | y | s | c | p | e | d | t |
| g | b | t | x | z | e | a | g | i | n | l | u | i |
| i | g | a | v | i | r | n | c | m | e | l | s | t |
| t | e | n | g | o | i | w | j | h | k | a | g | i |
| i | x | u | h | p | a | s | f | t | c | r | l | s |
| s | k | s | o | w | v | p | n | x | i | q | v | t |
| u | p | o | l | i | o | m | e | u | h | e | p | a |
| z | h | b | l | t | y | u | o | i | c | m | b | z |
| w | h | o | o | c | c | m | e | a | s | l | e | s |

**BONUS:**  Write the two words that appeared twice.

_____   _____

# Reader's Theater Script

*Reader's theater* is an exciting and easy method of providing students with the opportunity to perform a play while minimizing the use of props, sets, costumes, or memorization. Students read the dialogue of the characters or narrate from the book or prepared script. The dialogue may be read from the book just as the author has written it, or the teacher and students may create a new script. In a reader's theater production, everyone can be involved in some way. Encourage class members to participate even in off-stage activities, such as greeting the audience and helping behind the scenes. Production of the reader's theater makes an excellent culminating activity.

## How to Create a Script

1. Choose one of the following Miss Nelson books: *Miss Nelson Is Missing!*, *Miss Nelson Is Back,* or *Miss Nelson Has a Field Day.*

2. Read through the book again with the students.

3. Tell them that, together, they will write a new version of the book, using their own names as the "kids."

4. List the characters in the script. Include the following parts: narrators, Miss Nelson, Miss Viola Swamp, the kids (student's names), etc.

5. Follow the story line of the book from the beginning to the end, and together write a new dialogue to express the feelings of the "new kids" (students) in the script.

6. Copy the new script so each student has a copy. Highlight individual parts.

7. Encourage students to be expressive while reading the script.

   - There can be two casts. One can read the script, while the other pantomimes the actions of the characters.

   - All performers can stand with their backs to the audience. When a performer reads his or her lines, he or she turns, faces the audience, and reads the lines. When finished, he or she faces away from the audience.

## How to Make Simple Costumes

Although costumes are not necessary in a reader's theater production, your students may wish to wear simple costumes. Here are some other suggestions:

   - Use the script with the Miss Nelson and Miss Viola Swamp puppet characters that have been provided for you to use with the puppet theater (page 17). Have students create new "kids" puppets on the blank faces on page 18.

   - To create masks for the characters and themselves, have students refer to Masks! Masks! Masks! on page 39.

   - Visors can be made out of poster board and elastic. Draw a visor shape on poster board. Cut it out and staple a 4" to 6" (10 cm to 15 cm) piece of elastic to both ends of the visor. Draw the character and write his or her name on the visor.

# Alike and Different

Miss Nelson was the main character in the following three books: *Miss Nelson Is Missing!*, *Miss Nelson Is Back*, and *Miss Nelson Has a Field Day*. Each book has a different story. Read two or all three of the books, and write how they were alike and different.

**Alike**

_____

_____

_____

_____

_____

_____

**Different**

_____

_____

_____

_____

_____

_____

_____

# Bibliography

**Miss Nelson Books**

Allard, Harry (author) and James Marshall (illustrator). *Miss Nelson Has a Field Day.* Houghton Mifflin Co., 1985.

Allard, Harry (author) and James Marshall (illustrator). *Miss Nelson Is Back.* Houghton Mifflin Co., 1982.

Allard, Harry (author) and James Marshall (illustrator). *Miss Nelson Is Missing!* Houghton Mifflin Co., 1977.

**Books About Texas**

Capstone Press Geography Department. *Texas.* Capstone Press, 1996.

Thompson, Kathleen. *Texas: Steck Vaughn Portrait of America.* Steck-Vaughn Co., 1996.

Welsbacher, Anne. *The United States: Texas.* Aldo and Daughters, 1998.

# Answer Key

## Page 19

1. misbehave
2. unload
3. awful
4. polite
5. wonderful
6. part
7. open
8. agree
9. encourage
10. shout
11. play
12. sour

## Page 21

1. Marina Beech
2. Tim Chang
3. Daniel DeLeon
4. Demarco Hill
5. Haley Mekus
6. Anthony Morales
7. Stephen Sanford
8. Sara Sutton
9. Kelly Tikado

## Page 25

## Page 35

Verse 1—tell
Verse 2—shock wave
Verse 3—berserk
Verse 4—drill
Verse 5—rut
Verse 6—turn

## Page 38

1. $2.25
2. $2.80
3. $3.05
4. $2.85

## Page 40

1. bronchitis
2. gastritis
3. laryngitis
4. appendicitis

## Page 42

Stephen Sanford (63)
Anthony Morales (81)
Daniel DeLeon (30)
Tim Chang (15)
Demarco Hill (88)
Miguel Peterson (50)
Mike Ling (7)
Jason Greene (72)

## Page 43

1. Central Werewolves (Wins 12, Losses 0)
2. Anderson Mustangs (Wins 11, Losses 1)
3. Woodland Bulldogs (Wins 10, Losses 2)
4. Spindletop Oilers (Wins 9, Losses 3)
5. Terrell Wranglers (Wins 8, Losses 4)
6. Diablo Rangers (Wins 7, Losses 5)
7. Lasco Longhorns (Wins 6, Losses 6)
8. Estrada Broncos (Wins 5, Losses 7)
9. Halliday Cowboys (Wins 3, Losses 9)
10. Smedley Tornadoes (Wins 0, Losses 12)

## Page 44

1. 2 touchdowns, 2 one pointers
2. 2 touchdowns, 2 two pointers
3. 4 touchdowns
4. 5 field goals
5. 11 touchdowns, 11 one pointers

## Page 45

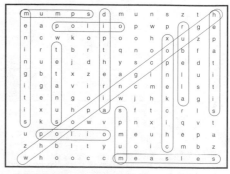

BONUS: mumps, polio